T0153321

Violet Energy Ingots

VIO ENE ING

Wave Books *Seattle / New York*

L E T

R G Y

O T S

Hoa Nguyen

Published by Wave Books

www.wavepoetry.com

Copyright © 2016 by Hoa Nguyen

All rights reserved

Wave Books titles are distributed to the trade by

Consortium Book Sales and Distribution

Phone: 800-283-3572 / SAN 631-760X

Library of Congress Cataloging-in-Publication Data

Names: Nguyen, Hoa, 1967–

Title: Violet energy ingots / Hoa Nguyen.

Description: First edition. | Seattle ; New York : Wave Books, [2016]

Identifiers: LCCN 2015043385 | ISBN 9781940696355 (limited edition hardcover)
  | ISBN 9781940696348 (trade pbk.)

Classification: LCC PS3614.G88 A6 2016 | DDC 811/.6—dc23

LC record available at http://lccn.loc.gov/2015043385

Designed and composed by Quemadura

Printed in the United States of America

9 8 7 6 5 4 3 2

Wave Books 058

AUTUMN 2012 POEM   1

DEAR LOVE NOT AS ONE,   4

MEKONG I   6

HAUNTED SONNET   8

A BRIEF HISTORY OF WAR   9

HEADLESS OR HEAD   10

WHO WAS ANDREW JACKSON?   11

A SEPTEMBER ELEVENTH POEM   12

SCREAMING   14

BIRTHDAY POEM   15

PHARAOH NOTES   16

WEEK OF WORDS   17

HOW THE SUN SHIVERS   19

AFTER SONNET 117   21

POEM OF FIRST LINES FROM JACK SPICER POEMS   22

STRUMMER   23

MEANT TO   24

SOME, VISITING   26

JANUARY	27
THREAD CORD	28
HAWK CHASED BY BLACKBIRDS	29
TOWER SONNET	31
MACHIAVELLI NOTES	32
DIANA WAS THE MOON	34
BLOUSY GUITAR	35
DIGRESSIVE PARENTHESIS	36
I DIDN'T KNOW	37
PS:	38
FIRST FLOWERS	39
THE WHITEBOARD	40
ORPHEUS POEM	42
LOCUST TREE NOTES (EAST TORONTO)	43
MY GREEN	45
I AM TOO	47
EAT VIOLETS	48
ANGEL GOING POW	49

MOAN & LOW   51

SHE SAILS (SPRING)   53

POEM OF FIRST LINES FROM TAGORE POEMS   54

HID   55

DO I PLUNGE   57

SUNFLOWER GUARDIANS   58

SPARROW AGAIN   59

BLOODLANDS   61

ARTIFACTS FROM THE "UNEARTHLY
CAVE" NAMED "THE PLACE WHERE
THE MAN WAS KILLED BY THE BULL"   63

AFTER THE MURDER BALLAD   64

TO SEEK   65

EVE   67

COPPER   68

DREAM IN OCTOBER   69

ME THAT   71

THE DIFFERENCE IS VELOCITY   73

FOR LOVE RED   74

RED VOICE   76

OWL   77

TORN   78

YOU   79

SONNET FOR MIMIR'S HEAD   80

AFTER THE SONG   81

AND   82

LEAVE   83

Acknowledgments   85

For Aphrodite, deathless and of the spangled mind

When shall I start to sing
A loud and idiotic song that makes
The heart rise frightened into poetry
Like birds disturbed? —Jack Spicer

Violet Energy Ingots

AUTUMN 2012 POEM

Call capable
    a lemony
light & fragile

Time like a ball and elastic

so I can stop burning the pots

wondering yes   electric stove

She is her   but I don't re-
member   remember
the ashes I obsess   She said

I was obsessed with
(not wanting to work with
ashes)

    Mandible dream
     says the street
& ash work

because the scorn
and ions long

there   I wor—   I woke up
in the overlooked dark

   I work
do that warp   twistingly
wrap the dead

Black and white like the
long-dead   starved pet rodent
eating the basement
        curtains and peanut shells

   I walk   I wal—
I walks down sometimes
why the advi—

abide   the advice was

not "Fair better"
but "Fail better"

Auto dish soap
½ and ½
Coffee beans

Bake the golden things
Rust colors
Rust colors

DEAR LOVE NOT AS ONE,

The tomatoes look like one-pound
ox hearts and impossible
you with soft strong arms (gift)

I lifted the skin and drank
the camping white wine
swirled into circles

    Am I the protected sheet
in between? The pines
strung with blue   protectively?

I think of you as pine crust
oak stairs   boys' feet   free
crystal center

We find red for vivid
fucking   red for birth
blood and my
tongue color

Captured me at first

I know   I'm not to be the center
sharply yellow(ish)

Why ask that we sing
        "Build me up

Buttercup, baby"
(just to let me down)

MEKONG I

River as sift
and sorter

Raw fruits and sell the wares
"Floating market"

Stone   pebble   sand
The silt and new islands

There were 9 mouths
9 dragons   but they change

as the letter is a triangle
She could be seen as

swan or generalized white
bird   Goddess that ate the earth

How to strand   become
mangroves   stranded

and braid your oiled hair

Vivid swoops that coil
a mouth and canal steered

Row from here to there

HAUNTED SONNET

Haunt lonely and find when you lose your shadow
secretive house centipede on the old window

You pronounce *Erinyes* as "Air-n-ease"
Alecto: the angry   *Megaera*: the grudging

Tisiphone: the avenger (voice of revenge)
"Women guardians of the natural order"

Think of the morning dream with ghosts
Why draw the widow's card and wear the gorgeous

Queen of Swords crown   Your job is
to rescue the not-dead woman before she enters

the incinerating garbage chute   wrangle silver
raccoon power   Forever a fought doll

She said, "What do you know about Vietnam?"
Violet energy ingots   Tenuous knowing moment

A BRIEF HISTORY

OF WAR

And what if Jupiter
is your faith

a balloon
but I call you

by the improper
names   I'm stained

by the world here
To be brave and endure

the losing   To be brave
and be the losing

Luck   Brutal

HEADLESS OR HEAD

Headless or head lowered   bowed down
I have legs   could club you where
The zygote lives   A love zygote
A zigzag stream in orange

What are these metallic squiggles
and yellow   that giant urge
to hover   The place of death
and lentil-burger dinner

Head down   golden golden
A blue explosion
crowned my head and wrung me out
Removed a tooth so I cleaned it

WHO WAS ANDREW JACKSON?

He was the seventh president of the United States
He was responsible for the Indian Removal Act
He was poor but ended up rich
He was an enslaver of men, women, and children
He was given the nickname "Indian killer"
He was put on the twenty-dollar bill

A SEPTEMBER ELEVENTH POEM

Can cry and alarm
the children

try to explainedness

despite Virgo birthdays
and pop music

of lineage past and future
to become crux of

"You seem mad at me"
(that's my boy to me)

Cry with an expat
expression   and strange tears after

   Cry for distant girlhood widowed friend

also many dead   alive   relatives

and what history   A colonial victory

                    fucked what-if
          fucked as if

SCREAMING

Screaming   mostly
I like to dance   dark woods
stony hills   lonely & moody
god   I can scream
floating piped tunes
mantle for protected onces

are]   possibly "all"

     etc.

You always "take me to yr hearts"
moonlit   sweet   after unearthly
whiskered tree-love   trusted
with my small horns
     mother-scorn

Such a mood flower   sequined
feet padding about

No   I do not want to see
pictures of your white progeny

BIRTHDAY POEM

Illuminated behind a skin
a grey   the sky with fat
fast slants of snow

Fire Horse poet   This is a birthday
poem   squeaky underfoot
the snow and Jeannine's cookies

I drive husbands and fathers
to early deaths   Push the knife
into the cake to cut it

Me the supposed bringer of ruin
(money)   Covered in fondant and
violet flowers

It's my birthday   My eyes are older

PHARAOH NOTES

Hatshepsut:
—sported a kilt and
bare chest

—wore a bull's tail
of gold & gems

—carried royal
crook and flail

—as a mummy she
is noted as "fat"

WEEK OF WORDS

Eyes for hearts
I mean   hearts for eyes

Words and words   choked on
Woody Allen anger grief

salt & vinegar popcorn

We watched *Winnie the Pooh*
        but only sort of

"Will I grow up to be cruel?"

No squares in your feelings

I washed the solo dirty shirt

Wiped the various surfaces
Peeled the nail

Snow all day
Snow all day

Killed for a meal
the Danish zoo giraffe
with redundant breeding genes

Wept in a bed
Explained the nature of 8s

Also grated cucumbers

Meet me in a dream bed
where I see your face

I dream I am yours to dread

HOW THE
SUN SHIVERS

In the poems
and that part of

off-key   my head
to store the limbo

The song
unless we hurt

it   where it shouldn't be
I form green

onions   Montage of
fire   bathe under

Here: each way
sweet   frizzled

as in fruit in candy
or "bear" called panda

(Just take it)
I run like an alehouse

run by a spider
Buffer cap

I mean buttercup   Fool
Sweet and butter sweet

Open up the sun
skipping over spring again

AFTER SONNET 117

I won't lawyer love   fish for blue
crabs with chicken necks tied to string
 o Love   how you plumb
and play down the spine of me   It's the bay
of my youth I'm drawn to   doing leg
lifts à la Jane Fonda on the wooden dock
Pink bathing suit in frays from a second season
 fraying   and I said from there   What you taught me
in dark eyes   the dream of you like a half-
born self of sun and rain   (cloud)   To braid myself
to braid to sunrise myself   a still-faced
one   But shoot me not   sting with the buried
arrow   To put among the stars   a constellation
(web of love?)   music   medicine   shooting

POEM OF FIRST LINES

FROM JACK SPICER POEMS

Baudelaire country Heat   Hills without gold
Be bop de beep
Because the figtree was sapless
Because they accused me of poems
Bewildered
Child
Coming at an end   the lovers
Damn them

STRUMMER

with apologies to Lindsey Buckingham

"Let the wolves run free" (moon)

Washed my hair   Spanish crocus
Serpent-bender stepping
                           on a heart fire

She said something about danger faces

Dear Kimberly—
I have asked for days
        my empty blue
                and leaves   trees in the rain

There's the tall tall grass
I've lain down in it
                doing my stuff

MEANT TO

Meant to cover the mouth
Silver strands now   and a cloak
Hair as long as yours   undone

Knocks from the Frigidaire   her
flee to seek
                    San Francisco

Eat red candy hearts

            Up from sleeping   wet hair
Sister could see her sticking

You leapt   Her beauty fell
fall of her   Helle was her name

Fall into seas   irretrievable

Cape to ash to mourn?   Her
or was the torch

Did you torch?

Your running

Did you turn when
your sister fell?

SOME, VISITING

Helpers here and bend down
landscaped in my waking

A sky ceiling   A natural tambourine
that rings and rattles

Also: snow
Also: a whoooing

"Unkinged by affection"
One little owl statuette

Count all the
ways to be undone?

We recall the lesser-known cryptids:
Owlman   Loveland Frog

Accidentally hit you hard
with my elbow

JANUARY

January long light
Janus   I see you
God of locks and doorways

two-faced looking in Capricorn
Capricious like the snowy owl
        irruption

We fear heavy body collisions

January   time of doors
time looking back on itself
    God of gates

    spelt and salt

They say when you
walk through a door

you can forget what
    you came for

THREAD CORD

Slipping over flowers
to the dead place
flame head   You make me salt again

I am comfortable with the couch
and a rather perfect Yule tree
with various red birds and glass baubles
plus "3rd-world"-made
lace snowflakes (crocheted)

Do you remember the feral
Siamese cat we named
Charles Bernstein?

Rage dented the silver
trashcan
              "fire-crack" or "schrack"

A new sun for the light of the world
back with you   again

HAWK CHASED BY BLACKBIRDS

You seek   the edge of the bed
and I dream where the sick one
needs a shot in the ass   a tricked shot
maybe have to set up the hypo
on the toilet seat for accidental
sitting-on of the cure

and you are late for your presentation
in which you discuss disaster aftermath

   The mother in the dream shows
her new baby with mismatched-sized eyes
and I pretend not to see

the Ghosts of Christmas Past   fall asleep
and found your mouth in a kiss

You can keep the beer

Faint face-whiskers
      Black beans on toast

I said   Fuck it   fold socks

The extension cord will not
        reach the light
wrapped around
the pear tree in white

TOWER SONNET

I offer it to chaos and writing
green pear my son brought me
A whole new country   a new
theater dream of you in a half-lit

maze   In the garden   why do I
and now collards and tomatoes
and new rain   glasses for reading
I got the drugstore kind

one of *those* dreams
You snicker as I pass   of course
and now smear the glass to see
and now a vehicle of teeth and smoke

and now stoop and tug on portals
no   not tugging   Old loose flood

MACHIAVELLI NOTES

Machiavelli conversant
in Italian and Latin (not
Greek)
      never had to have
"official income"

Middle height   black-haired
with a rather small head
reports of thin closed lips

             He sought after
much— Not really a life of leisure
      but of misfortune—

Took wrong side   was tortured
Proud to have passed the ordeal

Bored with the hicks on his farm

He gave himself readily
to "transient amours"

(A secret hero of mine)

Scorpio

DIANA WAS THE MOON

Full moon
that air between ears

Brutal was how I put it
You captive in the bathroom

I am staring   not starving
maybe starring   not scarring

I think this is instead a cancer
   cell proliferation

like the old dried hydrangea flower

I am indifferent to you
The indifference is practiced

BLOUSY GUITAR

Blousy guitar   I don't want to count the beats   Hey Hey
My pen   I have bed hair in the best way   Daughter
of sunlight and air   and I'm glad you were born
on this day or put another way: that you were

born   Let's be superstars   Let's call each other "suckas"
Turn everything into writing   Lord of my Love
and eat new raw oysters with many condiments
to lord & love   to be generally great

The flopping flowers that die in a poem
Summer solstice smacks me in the face   ridiculous
and I dream the different   like a naked sonnet
Your raw throaty laugh submerged under hot noodles

I wrote "valley" when I meant "longing"
Your laugh a river   A trout kind of green

DIGRESSIVE PARENTHESIS

Make heart-shaped cakes
for the Queen of Heaven

Things that make you cry:
Geode stone pulse

That plant named wizard's herb
When the state of Michigan sells

"pristine treaty-protected land"
to make a limestone mine

I dreamt the spider crossed
my eye and I crushed it

into my eye   Why is the first
day the hardest day?   The city

susurrus   Are us   especially
if you get to keep the money

I DIDN'T KNOW

I didn't know my milk
    could return   racing

to save the orphan baby
this morning with ghosts

      minor men   and shook
the tricky omnivorous bandit

before it could bite again
Truck exhaust enters the house

One hydrangea flower
    and leaves gust in the wind

on "my" side of the fence   (stolen)
The smooth cup is upheld by a brown

hand as if to say
    Today is the 70th anniversary

of the bombing of Hiroshima

PS:

for Marina Lazzara—from her note in October

If you get this
before you leave

take some California irises
home with you

Put in fridge until spring
Plant in circle

FIRST FLOWERS

Wasps out of the birdhouse
for spring   my boys shook
    out the dead wasps

New fly west
New fly west

for spring? To sip it?
Little gatherings of birds

Why does this feel like weeping?
    (snowdrops)

My friends   we love

It is two kinds of lost
that I'm lost in

THE WHITEBOARD

The whiteboard says "Vag Bleed"
I read *Anna Karenina*

If your mother is a waitress
   Trees   I gave them names

as a girl   The female ones
assigned "sad" and willow   Why

   Another with a white
beard

I hid the old dime there
silver sliver

Was her name Ida
with worn old feet

pennilessness & blue blankets
                (polyester)

All the time: goodbye to this
Extinguish   This extinguish

in the wrongest of places
You eat the moon

suns   or chase the chase here
Bell   Bell   mortal

ORPHEUS POEM

My songs sour and sweet
move rocks   Persuade
the dead not to keep me
underground
                    instead
to the new moon play
La la la la la di da   your black marble
throne

            Start/Stop

This means try & try
This means losing

                        way
head   my love   salt
sense

            Torn to pieces

You turn into rivers   to tease
and please
            the cry cry trees

LOCUST TREE NOTES
(EAST TORONTO)

Locust   black
also honey locust   less furrowed
      inedible for humans
Seeds eaten by squirrels   doves

They reestablish "disturbed sites"
with nitrogen roots
  amend soil

(my notes say *soul*)

Roped ridged bark
more furrowed with age

Fragrant flowers   white
      clusters hang down
Legume family   giant flower tutus

Native to Lake Erie
    area   not native here

Used to reclaim "damaged land"

Susceptible to
    native borer bug

MY GREEN

(my green grief)
I believed an open
mouth   I disobedience

informed by a spider   ushered
from an eye

Many pale green
peppers in the garden

and freak out
& fall down in a weep

I said my heart was a coal miner
cave-in   It was caved in
walking around

How to be
moving like words & magic

the true-blue song & damp
deck   & wet pussy

& the trees have leaves
shaped like a heart
heart-shaped leaves

We sent the spider
to the window for luck

I AM TOO

I am too much
      I am forever
too much   and every day
    you never come
        to my house

EAT VIOLETS

Like things that give a bitter feeling
and crush headaches   We seek bird

origin stories   I gentle you   if I do
with variegated stripes and yogurt

in plastic cups   Why money God trust?
Maybe we are exactly the chickens

and deserve a city like New York City
a swimming pool tango and cold fruit salad

I clock time   Violets you can eat
day/night   How to curl trees   Leave them

Pine swung   oak aloof
Branch down   chain saw down

"Wars are more fun with money"

ANGEL GOING POW

Pansies   the yellow-faced
pansies   bearded   & the robin
is a twerp
        twirping in the pear

Why do I say robins
are *not* my favorite?

Jays perch or pear   why jays
I hear the sun

        Do I hear sun?   I wrote
these lines after John Bell sees

We wondered together
whether the moon undoes the sun
like a pansy

& the robin busts about
        eating worms

No   this is not the start of something

North spring   gawd
like a gob-smacked sip   etc.
into spring wind

MOAN & LOW

after Libby Holman

What is this adding up to? A kind
of either/or   Kneel so bad

sick and warm   "I feel like
    miniature chocolates"

A kind of twirl inside   inside
    where you twirl the voice   Die perhaps

like a woman   nature-y
    purpling the hyacinth

                    (smells like purple)
I am in profile so you can

see my "good side"   3 smashed
birthday zinnias   a-la-di-la-da-die

groan   You know   the fun
        kind of mucus

In the future   there will be
no compulsory monogamy

SHE SAILS (SPRING)

I should like to king like the Troung sisters
Radicchio for the grail because you have to soak

alliance   Drown your long hair   (like in lost
like in lots of garlic and slicing in half)   Romances

goodbye   Lawn mowers groan and mustard garlic
grows   Circles where the syllables used to be

I said I'm at the threshold   which sounds
like something I would say

It's cold   It warms   It suns   It rains

POEM OF FIRST LINES
FROM TAGORE POEMS

Let me never lose hold of this shape
Let me never lose
Life of my life   I shall ever try
Light   my light   the world-filling light
Light   oh where is the light
More life   my love   yet more
Mother   I shall weave a chain of pearls
My desires are many and my pitiful cry
No more noisy   loud words from me

HID

Eels & water snakes
½ moon   the moon is halved
and I swear you are dead

The dead hang
        cormorant wings

We watch the special features
they grind   wheeling over Leslie Spit

Can mourn the dead of something
Denuded trees

Am mourning dead not dead

Little pied cormorant   (can write the dead)
"Shag"   (not dead)
Bald raven   (the one not dead)
Double-crested   (but wish dead)

Waterproof or preen gland secretions
My father after the river

Dear You
    etc.

I was born in the river
I have never known you   Father
Pacific Island fish eater

Hold my wrists to reason
Hold my rock neck

Hold my wings out still
My still-out wings

DO I PLUNGE

Hunched over to walk
drumming and where not
to enter the glass

Imagine Ezra without books
in the open-air "tiger cage"
rained-on   old
Aphrodite as a splay of hope

It's the last day of the Horse year
Does this mean the ass end
or a wisp of the tail?

My job is to put red-hot candies
into a pale-green bowl

It's true that I saw you
You were slashed with swords

SUNFLOWER GUARDIANS

Draw your name   many
times   stylized and
embarrassed

          Call them
catkins   yer name
writ there

Don't pull the wild
amaranth   I said

The old
Ford Galaxie 500 and cats
can guard the house

Who is crying
next to the thicket of birds?

I won't   I said   again
lick the ass   again
of the tyrant   again

SPARROW AGAIN

Why did I wake up singing "Judy
in Disguise"   rescuing the brown

baby from the ladder fall
from the swallowed grape

from being alone   too small
and motherless   asleep in my arms

Forget the strong delicate
difficulty   wearing a green shirt

chimney sweep sparrow

and the Little Debbie
cream-filled oatmeal cookies

each one wrapped in plastic

The dogwood tree dies   42 years old
    hunks of dried rice paper

Shake 'N Bake chicken

Cantaloupe eyes?
Lemonade pie?   Many cars later

"You made me a life of ashes"

BLOODLANDS

(First I wrote "bland lands")

Could be a score or map of the heart?
Where is "the heart"?   Hanging
above a doorway threshold   a fireplace
icon   full of impossible scars

"Love and Irony" is the name
of a small memoir

I toasted corn tortillas   melted
cheese   washed the pile of towels
and a white blanket that pills

Does the map include flaccid Florida?

We have plastic wine cups
            and plastic "microbeads"
from certain face & body wash
        also microplastic for the ocean
from daily washing machines

My house smells like spice and garlic
New moon Aries
       the one who hates enclosure

Fly and fly   with heavy wings

I should like to see a flower

ARTIFACTS FROM THE "UNEARTHLY CAVE" NAMED "THE PLACE WHERE THE MAN WAS KILLED BY THE BULL"

Bracelets
Pipes
Flints
Beads
A rusty knife blade
A shaving brush
An old flintlock horse pistol
A Canadian penny
A human skull with three holes in the forehead (white man)
A gold ring inscribed *A. L.*

AFTER THE MURDER BALLAD

Bring some other fine things
hard full life   atoms springing

No money   No fine things

Flatteringly   we are the cave
   It will be OK in disgrace

She jumped   Came to the river
deep water   Thou restless ungathered

orphan   Tell me your mind
to mend   to drown you in despair

                Let me sing gone
If I can live kicked & choked

Turned around in deep water

TO SEEK

To seek too much attention etc.
To be careful and mouth all the words
My glories are morning and purple

You too like a vine cling and closing
blue violet   ()

Marvin Gaye would sing

What is a Cry House for
(crying in the house)

I forgot why I wept
last night   It was children
& dark   I wear a silk
camisole   do I

and a cheap black
tunic

Here is a brown pastel scribble
and should be shamed

Can glitter? I show
off all the time

    Should start
dinner   and the surface is scored
the impressions trying too hard

I want the root of the words
not the fucking use
made purposed and stupid

Many any root feet be
May my root feet be

EVE

I could be naked and eating
figs   Instead I'm a rib-woman
howling and chased
by a winged god-baby

My man is embarrassed

                    kicked out
                    of the world-garden
                              to become farmers

COPPER

Copper is the metal of Aphrodite
(penny)

The goddess of Love but not fidelity

to press   to be newly born

"We are so odd"

"I think I just fell in love with everyone"

She found the lost & found
star bandanna square

To listen or to ride

the Dundas Square Ferris wheel
Raining rain

Snowflake
to my garnet lip   like streakiness

DREAM IN OCTOBER

Dream of childhood friend Wendy
casually exiting my apartment window
to jump to the rooftop deck
so we can perch and talk with city
views   but she is too casual
         and I see her miss
the landing   not jumping
far enough   an absolute plunge
ten stories down

    Her yelling regrets
        "Stop"   "O no   o no

I cover my ears so as not to hear the impact

Not to refer to widow   or want
to mention the dream scream
Frantic 9-1-1 dialing   I can barely

Let's leave it at this

Take the risk
Don't
Die
Impact
Children

ME THAT

Sing me that   sing me
this way   Terry-cloth bathrobe

stains on the collar
She asked me about shame

I said like a stain

Off and write my drugstore
reading glasses   this is new

o Philip Whalen   I have tatty fingers
clutter container arrangement and lack

of shelf liners   My kitchen cabinets
won't close (show poorly organized spices)

I spell dying in the boneyard
       The light in November dies

A hand from the dead on your leg
stabbed jean pants   the scared story

Our windows need hair dryer–
plastic treatment   healing less quickly now

The house drafts   My finger cuts

THE DIFFERENCE
IS VELOCITY

Name the ice
rime on the glass

insecty or bother
like glass on glass

Crack it now   but the mouse
ate through the protective

screen   We have to dump
this out and start over again

You weren't yourself then
Erase the playback

Compose the sonnets
or a sweetheart neck

Lace that you do not
garland for the charm

FOR LOVE RED

For love   red
roses were lost

   Loss
wake of
here   in the try
to be

You grow used
         Worn thumb
  an emblem of gone

and under new weather

Wet

  Want to say
     Wet her

I said

         Heart fells

Grow a mountain of snow

Eat the snow
    and a night of snow

RED VOICE

Empire seeks power   I wrote that
as "Vampire Empire" and drank hot

ginger tea and said I hate that shit
with a crying face eating potato soup

Smelly poetry I wanted vegetable
to make not like plaid but more rounded

and couldn't give the important internal
organ in a tawdry organ swap

Grey sky   a throat
How many many times to throw

I kissed her and pulled her
lower lip into my mouth

Venus hangs out with the moon
She said she wanted a baby

OWL

Water spirit owl
cold bird Libra moon
who said forever
and they lied   were an arm

Or is it a pink midsong world
owl who also means water moon
born of you like my sons emerged
as owl does each night   weighing matter

I don't mean to turn you
you who I love like poetry
trees bloom   tresses in the tree
          a pear blossoming

Your moon is flame   pink is
a flame of you tripled and a force
form   Owl said

Don't destroy your house
and run   small flattened pods
and seeds   Build your place in the trunk
the strongest place   (wavy-edged leaves)

TORN

Maybe the striped dress is named "Torn"
because of the angled stripes that don't match
up   Deep V-neck opening and a color called
"blue combo"

I lied to the white observers
in the dream when I said   "Someone
like me"   and I meant in my embodied
difference
             but instead made up a different
reason for the statement and applied gritty
cleaning scrub to my face

To be original is to arise
from a novel organ?

Born at dawn from a severed
circumstance

"Sorry   I won't apologize"

YOU

I cut the onions
You in the sun among
the multifarious faces
that open and color

(flowers)

How can one move
beyond doubt?

I felt or I felt I felt
i.e.: I am a striver
and could never smash
you   Catch my cloak

How are we bruised like
this blue   the sad
song   that one
and drown in you

1. Dink Roberts
2. John Snipes
3. Clarence Ashley

SONNET FOR MIMIR'S HEAD

Pooling the flesh and bind it
bid it be   It's your pool
I seek and sing   play
the guitar upside down

I was the song   pip in the tree
is a sustaining stutter star
inside your head   resides there
tells of the crackling   Hung:

The milk and country
A yell of living   No remedy for this
desire   *sín remedio*
especially the failed desire

without object   It aches right there
right there where the vocal slides

AFTER THE SONG

Descend the ladder
 don't write it down

An octopus with no arms

I used to wait
You shaving your face

What lasts
and clapping hands

A wilderness crescendo
 petal folds

tremble and I sign
my name   It's my
hand on the page

climb back up again

A chorus of screams
Sing   Sing the chorus again

AND

the plastic bottle cap in the dead
belly of the young bird

Albatross

LEAVE

Mouth   A pictured lip
in a kiss   What it leaves
out
      Cloaking your mouth
with your hands to say
no more breathing you in

Gather the firm clever thing
from the moment looking away

and the weather quiet
with the turning book

Bark of the trees
you love   then leave

Redbud
Live Oak
Hackberry

ACKNOWLEDGMENTS

Poems or versions of poems here previously appeared in print or online in the following venues: *Aesthetix, Argos Poetry Calendar 2013, Bat City Review, Bone Bouquet, The Brooklyn Rail, Capilano Review, Cedilla, Dreginald, Dusie, Eleven Eleven, EVENT, Fence, Granta, HUSH, The Lifted Brow, Likestarlings,* Literary Hub, *Los Angeles Review of Books, The Margins, Muthafucka, New American Writing, OAR,* PEN American Center, *Pinwheel, Plume,* Poets.org, *The Rusty Toque, Skidrow Penthouse, Sonora Review, Spolia, Summer Stock, Talisman, The Walrus,* and Woodland Pattern.

Some poems or versions of these were included in the chapbook *Tells of the Crackling* (Ugly Ducking Presse) and in the chaplet *Room Service* (Belladonna). Others were included in *Privacy Policy: The Anthology of Surveillance Poetics* (Black Ocean), *Please Add to This List: Teaching Bernadette Mayer's Sonnets & Experiments* (Tender Buttons), *Best American Experimental Writing 2014* (Omnidawn), and *The Sonnets: Translating and Rewriting Shakespeare* (Nightboat Books). The author wishes to extend her deep thanks to the editors and supporters of these poetry outlets.

Special thanks and gratitude are due to John Patsynski for his editorial eye on the poems.

Enduring love to my loves Dale Smith, Keaton, and Waylon.